black girls magic

coloring book

Copyright 2023 © Magge Hunt

ALL RIGHTS RESERVED. THIS BOOK OR ANY PORTION THEREOF MAY NOT BE REPRODUCED OR USED IN ANY MANNER WHATSOEVER WITHOUT THE EXPRESS WRITTEN PERMISSION OF THE PUBLISHER.

THANK YOU FOR PURCHASING OUR BOOK.

IF YOU ENJOY USING IT, WE WOULD APPRECIATE YOUR REVIEW ON AMAZON.
JUST HEAD ON OVER TO THE BOOK'S AMAZON PAGE AND CLICK
"WRITE A CUSTOMER REVIEW"

WE WALUE OUR CUSTOMERS AND ALWAYS WELCOME SUGGESTIONS AND FEEDBACK.

About this book

"Black Girl's Magic Coloring Book" is a unique opportunity to express yourself creatively and experiment with colors. You can let your imagination run wild by using different skin tones, creating unique designs for clothes and ornaments, and adding unique backgrounds and landscapes. This is your chance to create your own work of art and contribute to reflecting the diversity and beauty of black girls.

this coloring book belongs to

. . . .

color test pages

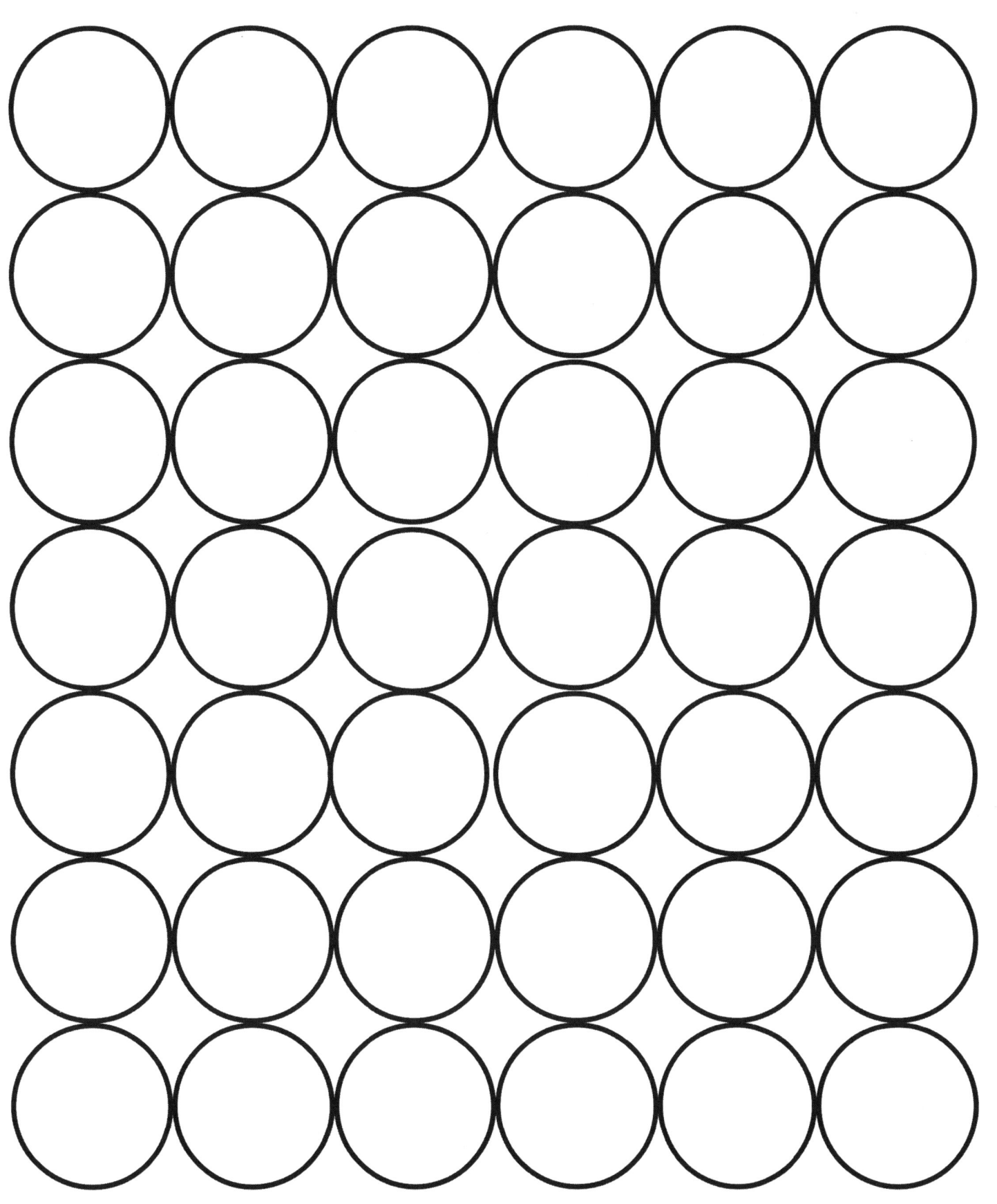

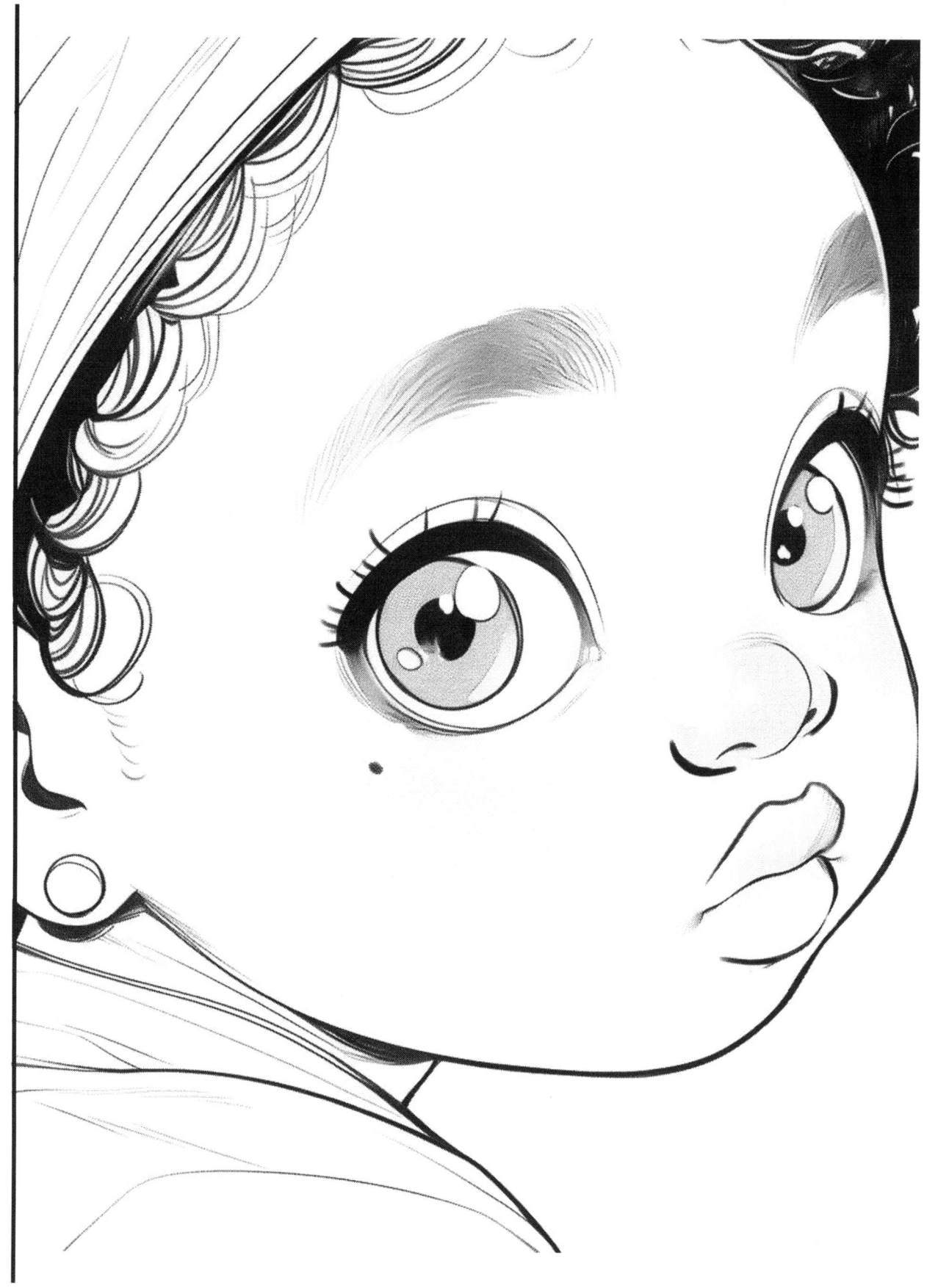

Made in United States
Troutdale, OR
10/22/2024